Ben Musgrave

Indigo Giant

With songs in English and Bangla by Leesa Gazi

Salamander Street

PLAYS

First published in 2024 by Salamander Street Ltd., a Wordville imprint. (info@salamanderstreetcom).

Indigo Giant Ben Musgrave, 2024

All rights reserved.

All rights whatsoever in this play are strictly reserved and application for performance etc. should be made before rehearsals to Ben Musgrave c/o. United Agents at 12-26 Lexington Street London W1F OLE. No performance may be given unless a license has been obtained. No rights in incidental music or songs contained in the work are hereby granted and performance rights for any performance/presentation whatsoever must be obtained from the respective copyright owners.

You may not copy, store, distribute, transmit, reproduce or otherwise make available this publication (or any part of it) in any form, or binding or by any means (print, electronic, digital, optical, mechanical, photocopying, recording or otherwise), without the prior written permission of the publisher. Any person who does any unauthorised act in relation to this publication may be liable to criminal prosecution and civil claims for damages.

Cover image by Caitlin Abbott

ISBN: 9781738429332

10 9 8 7 6 5 4 3 2 1

Further copies of this publication can be purchased from
www.salamanderstreet.com

Wordville

Indigo Giant is inspired by Dinabandhu Mitra's Nil Darpan, a trailblazing Bengali play that shook colonial India.

A Komola Collective production

WRITER'S NOTE

I lived in Bangladesh from the ages of eight to twelve. In 2016 I was commissioned by Jatinder Verma at Tara Arts to write a play in response to Dinabandhu Mitra's explosive *Nil Darpan* (*The Indigo Mirror*). Upon reading the play (which features psychopathic British planters crushing a Bengali farming family and community), I was profoundly shocked—firstly, because I had very little idea at all about the brutality of British planters in pursuit of indigo in Bengal, and secondly, because I had never seen 'the British' represented in this way. Reading *Nil Darpan* was like walking through a mirror and seeing the world from the other side.

The commission sent me on a research trip to Rangpur and Meherpur districts—visiting the sites of the old nilkuthis (indigo factories)—sinister, often ruined places. I was frequently told stories about how they were haunted by malevolent spirits from the time of indigo cultivation. This reminded me of the 'Indigo Giant' mentioned in *Nil Darpan*. I wondered: does the history of indigo cultivation still affect—or even 'haunt'—Bangladesh, a country changing and growing at an astonishing rate? And does the inspiring history of the Nil Bidroha—the extraordinary revolution that forced the planters out of Bengal—still speak to us today, in Britain, Bangladesh, India and beyond?

Indigo Giant has been an attempt to have a conversation between Britain and Bangladesh about this history. It's a story that we're trying to tell together. It's been a huge privilege to work with amazing Bangladeshi creatives and performers, as well as wonderful British creatives and performers, many of whom have heritage in Bangladesh and South Asia. This conversation, and this journey, has been led by Komola Collective, an astonishing arts organisation who have produced stunning productions of the play in Bangladesh and now Britain. I should also thank the University of East Anglia (especially RIN and HUM Impact and Research) for the many forms of support they have given this project over the last five years. Special thanks also to the Charles Wallace Trust. And also, of course, to Leesa Gazi, Jatinder

Verma, Selene Burn and my parents, without whom none of this would be possible.

There are too many others to thank than will fit in this note. Please see www.theindigogiant.com/acknowledgements for all the people and organisations who have supported and enabled this project.

Ben Musgrave

February 2024

KOMOLA COLLECTIVE

Komola Collective is an award-winning arts company dedicated to telling the stories that often go untold—stories from women's perspectives.

We are an award-winning ensemble of women from an array of creative and cultural backgrounds. We came together in 2013 to make exciting and engaging theatre that promotes female narratives and draws on a rich range of cultural influences. We create work that challenges social taboos and provokes discussion. We believe that through the arts we can spark social change. We are based in London, but our work takes us all over the world. So far our productions, films and outreach work have brought stories from different cultures to an audience of over 140,000 people in the UK and abroad.

We want to revisit history. Challenge social taboos. Unearth myths. Retell known stories. Question accepted beliefs.

Indigo Giant was supported using public funding by Arts Council England. At different stages, it has also been funded by a QR GCRF Rapid Response Fund Grant and grants from UEA's PVC Impact Fund, HUM Impact Fund, Impact Accelerator Award and an ISP Grant. The play was also generously supported by Redbridge Drama Centre, the Charles Wallace Trust and British Council Bangladesh. Fabrics were donated by Aranya.

Indigo Giant was first produced (in Bangla) at Mahila Samity in Dhaka, Bangladesh in September 2022.

The play was first performed (in English) at the Redbridge Drama Centre in February 2024, as part of a UK Tour, with the following cast:

Gopi / Supervisor:	**Chirague Amarchande**
Rashida / Mina / Nabina:	**Subika Anwar-Khan**
The Presence:	**Adi Roy Bhattacharya**
Kshetromani / Rupa:	**Amy Tara**
Rose:	**Thomas King**
Sadhu:	**Diljohn Singh**

The chorus was played by community ensembles in some of the cities on the tour. In Redbridge, these were: Anne Parveen, Mausumi Samanta, Ziaur Rahman. In Norwich, these were: Anne Tiburtius, Sherly Joseph, Alisha Kallarackal, Riya Vivek Thorat. In Birmingham, these were: Haleema Nasir, Prith Rathore, Tahsina Khan, Roji Sarkar.

Producer / Dramaturg:	**Leesa Gazi**
Director:	**Gavin Joseph**
Designer:	**Caitlin Abbott**
Music / Sound Designers:	**Sohini Alam** and **Oliver Weeks**
Lighting Designers:	**Nasirul Haque Khokon** and **Joe Price**
Assistant Director:	**Prashant Tailor**
Associate Producer:	**Pauline Nakirya**
Co-producer:	**Redbridge Drama Centre**
Co-producer:	**Ben Musgrave** and **Riot in the Light.**
Movement Director:	**Ching Ying**
Stage Manager:	**Sophie Meikle**
Production Manager:	**Sean Laing**
Videography:	**Alex Unai Arrieta**
Marketing and PR:	**Suman Bhuchar** and **David Burns**
Social Media:	**Aranyo Aarjan**
Researcher:	**Annie Zaidi**

ABOUT THE CAST AND CREATIVES

Diljohn Singh | Actor *(Sadhu)*

Diljohn recently finished filming a lead role in the feature film *Flight into Fear* and appears in the new Matthew Vaughn movie *Argylle* to be released in Spring 2024. Other screen work includes *Rickshaw, Great Britain, Boiling Point* with Stephen Graham, *Agatha Raisin: The Walkers of Dembley* and several Bollywood features including *Jawaani Jaaneman* and *Shiddat*. On stage, Diljohn appeared in *Hedda Gabler* at the Maltings Theatre, St Albans and *The P Word* (Vienna Theatre Project).

Amy Tara | Actor *(Kshetromani / Rupa)*

Amy is a Mixed Race British Indian actor, who enjoys hobbies such as horse-riding, fine art, chess and singing. Amy is also well travelled, being born in Dubai and living in places such as Australia. She feels being a part of the dramatic arts has uncovered so many hidden aspects of herself, and feels completely devoted and compelled to be part of a profession that bursts with enthusiasm, charisma, whimsicality and camaraderie. Amy credits include; Lumi in *The Snow Queen*, Matilda in *The Visit*, Christa in *12 Days of Christa*, Amara in *Out of Time, Out of Mind* (an original play), Mollie in *Young Love* and Sianna in *Vignettes*. On screen, Amy has had the privilege of playing Ivy in *One Time Deal* with the BFI Film Academy and, in 2024, Chloe in *Assassins Guild* on Amazon Prime.

Chirague Amarchande | Actor *(Gopi / Supervisor)*

Chirague Amarchande is a professional dancer and choreographer turned actor. He's experienced across TV, movies, commercials, stage and other mediums, leading him to work with Akram Khan, Mavin Khoo, Jay Sean, Gucci, Edgar Wright and others. Outside of performing, he enjoys exploring cuisines and places, reading, cooking and socializing. He loves the theatre and is delighted to be part of *Indigo Giant*.

Adi Roy Bhattacharya | Actor *(The Presence)*

Adi Roy Bhattacharya (he/him) is an actor based in London. His recent credits include: *The Tempest* (CSSD), *Blood Wedding* (CSSD), *WOMAN.LIFE. FREEDOM* (Camden Fringe'23), *The Trap: India's Deadliest Scam* (BBC), *Harmonium Melodies* (Brady Arts Centre). Training: The Royal Central School of Speech and Drama.

Subika Anwar-Khan | Actor *(Rashida / Mina / Nabina)*

Subika Anwar-Khan is a writer and actor who has appeared in various plays such as *Hear Me Now* (Theatre503), *Mephisto [A Rhapsody]* (Gate theatre), *Julie* (National Theatre), *60 Miles by Road or Rail* (Royal and Derngate) and *OK Tata Bye Bye* (Curve Theatre). She has also appeared in TV shows *Eastenders* (BBC), *Goldie's Oldies* (Nickelodeon) and Bafta winning feature film *After Love* (BFI).

As a writer Subika was a part of The Royal Court and Hampstead Theatre's writing programmes. She has developed scripts with Paines Plough, Curve Theatre, Tamasha, Belgrade Theatre, Birmingham Rep, The Roundhouse, Nabokov and Drywrite. Her plays have been produced by Kali Theatre (**** *The Independent Stateless*) and the Vault Festival (**** *Exeunt Magazine Princess Suffragette*). She was the writer and performer of solo show *Divided*, commissioned by Camden People's Theatre and *Echo*, her second solo show developed with Tara Theatre. Subika is published in *Hear Me Now* Vol.2 and was a contributing writer for audio drama *Beneath Our Feet* (Spotify, Apple Podcasts).

Thomas King | Actor *(Rose)*

Tom graduated from Rose Bruford College of Theatre and Performance in 2017. Since then he has performed a variety of roles in children's, actor-musician and immersive shows. His most recents credits include: *Secret Cinema presents Wishmas* playing the role of Wishkeeper/ Father Christmas, *FIT: The Musical* playing drums in the band, *Secret Cinema presents Grease* playing the role of Bobby the Prank Master and *Billy the Kid* playing drums in the band.

Leesa Gazi | Dramaturg, Lyricist, Producer

Leesa Gazi has dedicated her career to presenting stories from women's perspectives. She co-founded Komola Collective. Gazi directed the multi-award-winning docu-film *Rising Silence*, following the lives of wartime rape survivors of the Bangladesh Liberation War. Amazon Crossing published Gazi's acclaimed novel *Rourob*, titled *Good Girls* (tr. Shabnam Nadiya) in 2023. Gazi's debut feature, *Barir Naam Shahana*, recently won awards at the Jio MAMI Mumbai Film Festival and BFI LIFF 2023.

Ben Musgrave | Playwright and Co-producer

Ben Musgrave grew up in Britain, Bangladesh and India.

Pretend You Have Big Buildings won the inaugural Bruntwood Prize and was performed in the main house of the Royal Exchange Theatre, Manchester, in July 2007. Ben was subsequently commissioned by the National Theatre. Since then, he has been commissioned and performed many times. Highlights include *Breathing Country* (2009), for Y Touring, (shortlisted for the Brian Way award for Best New Play for Young People). *His Teeth* (2011), for Only Connect, was *Evening Standard* and *Time Out* Critics' Choice and was nominated for an Offwestend.com award for the best new play. *Crushed Shells and Mud,* which was developed on attachment at the NT Studio, opened at the Southwark Playhouse in 2015 and starred Alex Lawther. *Indigo Giant*, initially commissioned by Tara Arts, was workshopped at the National Theatre Studio in 2017 and produced in Dhaka, Bangladesh in 2022 before this UK tour in 2024. He also writes for other media, including radio and film. His last radio play, *Vital Signs,* was broadcast on BBC Radio 4 in 2022. He teaches on the MA in Scriptwriting at the University of East Anglia.

Gavin Joseph | Director

Gavin's theatre credits include Assistant Director for *The Glee Club* (Out of Joint), *The Unfriend* (Chichester Festival) and *The Way Old Friends Do* (Birmingham Rep). As a director, Gavin's credits include *Ad Nauseam* (Lyric Hammersmith), *Madam Interpreter* (Stanley Arts), *Hello, it's me* (Tamasha), *Little Threads* (Selladoor) and *For One More Day To Live* (Peckham Theatre). Gavin has previously worked as an Associate Artist at Company Three, where he was involved with writing and directing new pieces of work in collaboration with young people from Islington. Gavin has worked extensively with young people as a director and facilitator at various theatres including Southwark Playhouse, Wimbledon Civic Theatre Trust, The Kiln, Lyric Hammersmith and The Old Vic where he has also been an Artist Consultant. Gavin is an alumni of the Young Vic's Directors programme, Lyric Ensemble, National Youth Theatre, RADA Youth Company, Soho Sketch Lab and the Hackney Empire's Writers Room.

Pauline Nakirya | Associate Producer

As an actor and writer, Pauline is drawn to stories challenging norms and exploring human complexity. Her producing journey started in theatre, leading a youth group, adapting folktales, and performing solo. Transitioning to film, she joined Komola Collective, Line Producing *Barir Naam Shahana*, depicting a divorced woman's ostracism, and co-producing *I Am Light*, reflecting on black British identity post-George Floyd. She was Producer on *These Things Ain't Mine*, a dance film unveiling a former gymnast's abuse in British Gymnastics. Her work delves into societal issues, amplifying voices and narratives often overlooked in mainstream media, fostering empathy and understanding.

Prashant Tailor | Assistant Director

Prashant Tailor (he/him/his) is a South-Asian storyteller who aims to change the definition, function and cultural association of theatre. Keen on working with new writing that champions underrepresented communities, Prashant also carries an artistic flair for revolutionizing classics. His working-class background influences both his cinematic style of theatre-making and mission to make staged productions competitive against TV series and movies. Training as a director under Young Vic, Tamasha Theatre Company and Mercury Theatre, Prashant's recent theatre credits include: Assistant Director, *Cinderella* by Teresa Burns (Watford Palace Theatre), Director, *Don't Worry About Me But I Worry About You All The Time* by Kiran Benawra (The Nursery Theatre), and Director, *Manfred* by Mohamed-Zain Dada (Birmingham Hippodrome and Theatro Technis).

Caitlin Abbott | Designer

Caitlin was a Linbury Prize Finalist and an RSC Assistant Designer 2019-2020. Design credits include: *Houdini's Greatest Escape* (New Old Friends), *Roald Dahl's Revolting Rhymes* (Opera Holland Park, Waterperry Opera Festival), *A Single Man* (Park Theatre), *Time and Tide (*Norwich Theatre Royal), *Black, el Payaso* (Arcola, Cervantes Theatre), *Crimes on Centre Court* (New Old Friends, Theatre Royal Bath), *The Selfish Giant; Hamelin* (TRBTS, The Egg), *Autumn Opera Scenes* (Guildhall School of Music and Drama), *Perspective* (National Theatre, New Views), *Valentina Star Dreamer* (Haste/The Place), *The Elephant Man* (Bristol Old Vic).

Sohini Alam | Music and Sound Co-designer

Sohini Alam is a British Bangladeshi singer whose musical repertoire includes folk, modern and traditional Bengali songs. She also composes and has branched out into multi-lingual music in bands, dance, film and theatre. Sohini is the lead vocalist for the critically acclaimed bands Khiyo, Lokkhi Terra and In Place of War's GRRRL. She is the Musical Director of the arts company Komola Collective. A third-generation vocalist from a family of famed Bangladeshi singers, Sohini has provided vocals for dancer/choreographer Akram Khan's *DESH*, *Father*, and *Until the Lions*. She and her Khiyo bandmate Oliver Weeks are music directors of Leesa Gazi's multiple-award-winning documentary *Rising Silence* and the feature film *Barir Naam Shahana*.

Oliver Weeks | Music and Sound Co-designer

Oliver Weeks is a London-based composer, guitarist and pianist. He studied music at Clare College, Cambridge, and composition with Robin Holloway, followed by a PhD in composition from the Royal Academy of Music, London. His music has been performed by the London Philharmonic Orchestra, the Philharmonia, the Royal Academy Soloists and the BBC Singers. He has scored several full-length feature and short film soundtracks, including *Cat Sticks* (Ronny Sen, India 2019) and *Barir Naam Shahana* (Leesa Gazi, Bangladesh/UK 2023). In 2007, he founded the band Khiyo with Sohini Alam, ARC Music releasing their two albums in 2015 and 2022.

Sean Laing | Production Manager

Sean is a Production Manager for opera, theatre and events who trained at The Royal Central School of Speech and Drama. He regularly works with Pegasus Opera Company, Hampstead Garden Opera and the National Youth Theatre. Recent Production Manager credits include: *Ruth/Six of Calais*, *The Aspern Papers* (both Pegasus Opera Company), *DROWNTOWN – China* (Rhiannon Faith Company), *Hansel and Gretel*, *Agrippina*, *The Cunning Little Vixen* (all HGO), *Bluebeard's Castle* (Green Opera), *Acis and Galatea/Dido and Aeneas*, *Roald Dahl's Revolting Rhymes*, *Figures in the Garden* (all Waterperry Opera Festival), *The Winston Machine* (Kandinsky), *Ada, Playing Up 2022 & 2023* (National Youth Theatre), *Pigs Might Fly* (DEM), *Redemption, Mission* (both The Big House). Recent Deputy/Assistant credits include: *The Choir of Man* (UK Tour & West End). Recent Events Production Management includes: *London Film Festival XR Programme* (DDA Live for The British Film Institute).

Nasirul Haque Khokon | Lighting Co-designer

Khokon is the Principal Designer for Creations Unlimited Lighting & Visual Design and has been a lighting designer for over 25 years. His fascination with lighting led him to research the field, experiment with new technologies and push their boundaries. He uses light as a medium to reveal and accentuate, a way to play with the senses, emotions and reactions. Khokon considers the light as a means to embellish an environment or to strengthen perception and a message, maximise contrast and the evocative power of a setting, and develop iconographical and descriptive languages.

Sophie Meikle | Stage Manager

Sophie is a freelance stage manager based in London. She is a graduate of the Royal Central School of Speech and Drama. Previous Stage Management credits include: *Fairytale on Church Street* (The Cockpit), *A Christmas Carol* (Bridge Theatre), *Sarah* (The Coronet Theatre), *Tiger is Coming* (The Coronet Theatre), research and development projects for Vital Xposure, Industry Showcases for Rifco Theatre Company and Royal Central School of Speech and Drama. Film and television credits include: *The Power* (Amazon Prime & Sister Productions), *Killing Eve* (BBC America), *Infinite* (Paramount Pictures), *Cobra* (Sky Studios). Sophie grew up in India between the ages of 7 and 11 and is interested in theatre that celebrates South Asian culture.

Joe Price | Lighting Co-designer

Joe studied at the Royal Welsh College of Music & Drama and is now based in Bristol. He received the 2015 Francis Reid Award for Lighting Design and his work on *A Woman Walks Into A Bank* at Theatre503 was nominated for the 2023 Offie Award for Lighting Design. Credits include: *My Name Is Rachel Corrie* (Young Vic), *Outlier* (Bristol Old Vic), *Petula* (National Theatre Wales), *The World's Wife* (WNO), *Redefining Juliet* (Barbican), *Wendy, Five Children And It, Rapunzel* (TRB, The Egg), *Revealed* (Tobacco Factory), *Heads Will Roll* (Told by an Idiot), *Heather* (Bush Theatre), *Daughter of the Forest* (Komola), *Mrs Dalloway, Carmen, How To Date A Feminist* (Arcola Theatre), *Fossils* (Brits off-Broadway NYC).

Ching Ying | Movement Director

Ching Ying is a Taiwanese freelance dance artist based in London. Besides choreographing her own creations, she collaborates with other artists in different art forms. She has worked with Akram Khan Company since 2013. Her performance in *Until the Lions* won Outstanding Female Performance (Modern) at the 2016 National Dance Awards (UK). She is also a rehearsal director and company repertoire workshop teacher with Akram Khan Company. In 2020, she started working with James Thierrée-Compagnie de Hanneton in the creation of *Mo's* and *ROOM*. Her solo choreography piece *Vulture*, made in 2018, has performed in Europe and Taiwan. It also been selected as one of twenty pieces in Aerowave 2023.

Aranyo Aarjan | Social Media

Aranyo Aarjan is a London-based writer, climate change activist and bartender. His work has been published by Verso Books, Jacobin and Red Pepper magazine.

Ben Musgrave

Indigo Giant

With songs in English and Bangla by Leesa Gazi

CHARACTERS

THE PRESENCE

SADHU
(age 23)

KSHETROMANI
(age 23)

ROSE
(age 24)

NABINA
(age 24)

GOPI
(age 40)

RASHIDA
(age 25)

RUPA
(age 24)

JEREMY
(age 35)

SUPERVISOR
(age 40)

Farmers and Villagers

A Chorus

The play can be performed with a cast of six. In the UK production, a Community Ensemble played the farmers, villagers and Chorus.

ACT ONE: PARADISE

THE CLAY LAND

The present day.

A field in Bengal, gloriously green. It is hot.

Within the field, a bel tree. Silence.

PRESENCE: Listen?
It's quiet now.
There's peace.
The Sun
The Green.
The Soil.
A Tree.
For a moment, this feels like paradise.
As if nothing has changed since the dawn of time.
But do you remember?

Do you remember, what happened here?

Some farmers enter, singing:

CHORUS: O father come let us go
To the field to plough,
Place the ploughs on oxen shoulders
And push, push, push.
My wife has hanged herself
She could no longer bear hunger,
Now I plough deep into soil
In hope of seeing her again.
The giant is coming. The Daitya!
Don't you hear it? The Daitya!
Can't you hear the footsteps all around?
The Indigo Giant is coming!

আসেন গো পিতা, দেন গো যাইতে
(ASHEN GO PITA, DEN GO JAITEY)
মাঠে গিয়ে লাঙ্গল চষাই
(MATHEY GIYE LANGOL CHOSHAI)
বলদের কাঁধে জোয়াল বসাই
(BOLODER KADHEY JOWAL BOSHAI)
আর দিনমান হট-হট হট-হট
(AAR DONOMAAN HOT-HOT HOT-HOT)
বাঁই বাঁই বাঁই
(BAI BAI BAI)

পরিবার মোর ফাঁসিতে ঝুলে
(PORIBAR MOR PHSHITEY JHULEY)
সইতে না পেরে অনাহার,
(SHOITEY NA PERE ONAHAAR)
মাটির নিবিড়ে চষি হাল
(MATIR NIBIRE CHOSHI HAAL)
চালাই লাঙ্গল-জোয়াল
(CHALAI LANGOL JOWAL)
"যখন ক্ষেতে বসে ধান কাটি
(JOKHON KHTEY BOSHE DHAAN KATI)
মোর মনে জাগে ও তার নয়ান দুটি"
(MOR MONE JAGEY O TAR NOYAN DUTI)
আশায় আশায় থাকি, তারে যদি দেখি আবার
(ASHAI ASHAI THAKI, TAREY JODI DEKHI ABAR)

ঐ আসে রাক্ষুসে, দানব, দানব!
(OI ASHEY RAKKHUSHEY, DANOB DANOB)
শুনতে কি পাও না? দানব দানব!
(SHUNTEY KI PAU NA DANOB DANOB)
পাও না কি শুনতে পায়ের আওয়াজ চারিপাশে?
(PAU NA KI SHUNTEY PAYER AOWAJ CHARIPASHEY)
নীল দানব ছায়া ঐ আসে, ঐ আসে!
(NEEL DANOB CHHAYA OI ASHEY, OI ASHEY!)

The PRESENCE acknowledges the farmers.

PRESENCE: How is the land this year?

FARMER 1: The same as the last.

Pause.

PRESENCE: Do you grow what you choose to?

FARMER 2: Of course, we choose what we grow.

PRESENCE: Is your soil still healthy?

FARMER 1: Yes.

PRESENCE: Are you still healthy?

FARMER 1: Why do you ask all these questions?
If you ask any more questions like this we will tell you to leave.

The PRESENCE raises his hands in a gesture of reconciliation.

PRESENCE: Do you know what happened here? In these fields?

FARMER 1: No, we don't know anything.

PRESENCE: Do you know anything of the history?

FARMER 1: No, we don't know that history.

FARMER 2: It's too long ago.

FARMER 1: British?

FARMER 2: British?

FARMER 1: Maybe the old men will know.

FARMER 2: There are some men in the village who are 80,
maybe they will help you.

FARMER 1: I think even they will not know.

FARMER 2: Forgive us, Sir, we must go.
We have no time, today.
We are...

Beat.

The PRESENCE releases them. The farmers exit.

PRESENCE: There will be time.
There will be time.

The PRESENCE beckons KSHETROMANI and SADHU from the earth.
Though they are poor, they are dressed in wedding finery.

(*Of KSHETROMANI*) This is Kshetromani Haldar.
There was once a time when she charged round her father's fields.
Until he died.
There was a time she could challenge the universe.
And there will be time, again, I think.

(*Of SADHU*) This is Sadhu Charan. A tenant farmer. A raiyat.
He will hardly leave a trace in any record book.
But he is not nothing.
Because Sadhu Charan will plant something.
Something that will grow.

(*Of the bride and groom*) Of these two
She is greater than he.
But he is not nothing.

SADHU AND KSHETROMANI

1859. The Field. SADHU and KSHETROMANI, just married. There is an earthen hut on an earthen porch.

SADHU: It is here.

KSHETROMANI looks at the earthen home. It is more modest than she had imagined.

You are welcome, here.

She cannot bring herself to look.

There is not much to see.

She looks inside.
She comes out again, trying to hold back her disappointment.

I know it is not much.

But there will always be rice.
I am clean.
After the rains, I can take the walls out a little.
In case
Forgive me, I do not know
In case we need more /room

KSHETROMANI reflexes—it's too soon to talk about that!

SADHU: I'm sorry!

She looks away.

I am not so skilled.
In the ways of marriage.
(*Of her outfit*) I have never seen such finery!

Pause.

She takes off a bracelet and offers it to him.

KSHETROMANI: You should take it.

SADHU: (*Gently*) No, they are yours.

KSHETROMANI: You got nothing.

SADHU: I did not ask for anything.

She holds it out to him.

SADHU: We are not in any need.

KSHETROMANI: What do you want me to do? As your wife.

SADHU: You will cook?
Nothing rich.
And washing.
And sometimes, in the fields

KSHETROMANI: You wish me to work in the fields?

SADHU: Is it fine?

Pause.

KSHETROMANI: Yes, it's fine.

There are some little Krishnanagar clay figures in a corner of the hut. They catch her eye. He goes to pick one up.

SADHU: My father liked to make them.

He embarrasses.

I will keep them away.

KSHETROMANI: There is no need, when there is no other ornament.

This isn't going well.

SADHU: Do you like bel?

KSHETROMANI: I do not think much of bel.

SADHU: Look up?
My father planted this tree.
Bel.

He climbs the tree; he plucks a bel (wood apple).

Here.

He makes to toss her the fruit.

KSHETROMANI: (*Not wanting to catch it*) No!

He tosses her the fruit. She catches it. He climbs back down, rapidly, takes the fruit from her, and cracks at its circumference with his kazla (sickle). It opens—unveiling the strange seething delicious fruit. She smiles as she eats it.

SADHU: My father used to sing to this tree when it was a sapling. He would sing for hours. I still sing to it sometimes.

KSHETROMANI: What song?

SADHU: Love songs.

KSHETROMANI: Why?

SADHU: It is good practice.

KSHETROMANI: For what?

SADHU looks down awkwardly.

SADHU: Kshetromani. This land is blessed.

They listen to it. They hear a bird call and he sings back to it, and it responds.

There! I told the kokil you had arrived!

She admits a tiny smile.

He says he likes you!

She calls back. The Kokil calls back.

He says he will help you, any time you call for help.

SADHU: We will grow peaj this year.
We will grow aloo.
We will grow dhaerosh.
We will have an orchard.
We will have pineapples, mangoes, boroi, bel.

She sees the indigo plant.

KSHETROMANI: And indigo?

Pause.

SADHU: And indigo, yes.

He goes to an indigo plant with some water.

SADHU: *(talking to the plant)* We're nearly there!
There—you can drink now. Take on all the water you can.

He examines a plant. Looking at it gently.

I think you will make the most beautiful blue.
Like midnight.
Like Krishna.

KSHETROMANI: How much land do you give to indigo?

SADHU: Three bighas.

KSHETROMANI: *(concerned)* Three bighas is too much.
Are you in debt to him?

SADHU: *(Gently)* We do not have those problems here.

She turns away, sadly.

I am sorry. Kshetromani, for the sorrow of your family. But it happens sometimes. That a family cannot pay its debts.

Pause.

She goes over to the indigo plant. She reads it.

KSHETROMANI: The crop looks strong. The leaves are in good colour.

SADHU: You read the plant like a farmer.

KSHETROMANI: You took an advance from the Planter?

Beat.

SADHU: The terms were fair.

KSHETROMANI: How much was the advance?

SADHU: Thirty rupees.

KSHETROMANI: At?

SADHU: Three rupees a bundle.

KSHETROMANI: You think you can supply ten bundles?

SADHU: Yes.

KSHETROMANI: And if you are in shortfall?

SADHU: The planter here, Cameron Lovegrove, he is a good man.
He loved my father.
They used to sit at the Bungalow and smoke a pipe together and talk of soil.

9

The soil here is the best in the world.
He was to come to our wedding.

KSHETROMANI: But he did not come?

Pause.

They both feel a twinge——something not quite right.

SADHU: Kshetromani.
Our village is beautiful.
The people are kind.
We gather to sing sometimes, at the Kuthi.
The nights are soft.
A fire.
The stars.
The river.
The land breathing.
This is not the end of your life.

The two of them. Will a closeness form?

POOR MR LOVEGROVE

It is a new day. KSHETROMANI is inside the hut. SADHU sits thoughtfully on his porch. A villager, RASHIDA, walks by.

RASHIDA: Hoy! Sadhu Charan!

SADHU: Rashida-sister!

RASHIDA: How was your wedding night?

SADHU isn't quite sure what to say.

RASHIDA: Was it successful?

SADHU inclines his head: 'she is inside'.

RASHIDA: Are you happy?

SADHU: Yes, I am happy.

Beat.

RASHIDA: Sadhu——I have some news.
Your friend. The planter.

SADHU smiles.

SADHU: Mr Lovegrove.

RASHIDA: He died, Sadhu.

Pause.

RASHIDA: He had a fever. It came upon him in the night.

SADHU: Mr Lovegrove?

RASHIDA: The missionary has come to take his body to the church.
We do not know what will happen now.

SADHU: Mr Lovegrove is dead?

KSHETROMANI comes out.

RASHIDA: Sister!

KSHETROMANI: What is it?

Pause.

SADHU cannot speak. He turns away from her.

RASHIDA: Should we be worried, Sadhu?

Pause.

SADHU: No, don't be worried!
The Planters here, they have always looked after us.
They know how good our plant is.
They know it is the best in the world.
Look how good the plant is today!

But KSHETROMANI is not so sure. Somewhere, in the universe, there is a note off.

WE DO NOT REMEMBER ANYTHING

The FARMERS of today gather again, with The PRESENCE.

We are near the ruins of an old Nilkuthi.

Construction noise, close by. The PRESENCE listens.

PRESENCE: Hey! Brother! What have they built, over there?

FARMER 2: Garments factory.

PRESENCE: A factory?

PRESENCE: They chose to build a factory in the ruins of that place?
Don't you know what happened there?

FARMER 1: No, we don't know anything.

FARMER 2: Maybe the old men will know.

FARMER 1: They are only ruins.

FARMER 2: (*Pointing*) We do not know about those ruins. We do not pass them. Why should we know about them?
They are only stones and moss and weeds.
We do not go in there.

PRESENCE: Why not?

Pause.

How do you feel about this place?

FARMER 1: How do I feel? What kind of question is
It is not a question/ I can answer.

FARMER 2: It is a bad place.

PRESENCE: In what way is it a bad place?

FARMER 2: There are ghosts.

Pause.

FARMER 1: Yes, it is true, there are ghosts here.

PRESENCE: What kind of ghosts?

FARMER 2: Giants

PRESENCE: Giants? What kind of Giants?

RUPA enters.

FARMER 2: White Giants.
One night I was troubled by noises coming from the ruins of the kuthi, and I went to see them.
They screamed at me, the Giants, they told me not to look but I wanted to look. And I wished I had not seen. I wished I had not seen what I had seen. And they did this to me.

He peels off his eye-plaster, to reveal that he is blinded in one eye.

RUPA: Don't talk such nonsense...

FARMER 1: The kobiraj says it spellbound his leg.

RUPA: It's just superstition.

FARMER 2: (*Of RUPA*) She works at the factory.

FARMER 1: She was all high and mighty——full of plans...
But her land is not fertile anymore.

RUPA gives the FARMERS 'evils'.

PRESENCE: You work in the factory?

The PRESENCE perceives her. Is she who they've been looking for?

CHORUS: Brick-dust, sand, stones
Don't remember a thing any more
Nilkuthi is worn-out of indigo poison
A new trade is built with old stones
New income, known exploitations

সুর্কি, বালু, ইট, পাথর
(SHURKI, BALU, EET, PATHOR)
কিছু নাই স্মরণে মোর
(KICHHU NAAI SHORONEY MOR)
নীলকুঠি নীলে জর্জর
(NEELKUTHI NEELEY JORJOR)
সেই পাথরে নতুন কারবার
(SHEI PATHOREY NOTUN KARBAR)
পুরান শোষণ নয়া রোজগার
(PURAN SHOSHON NOYA ROJGAAR)

THE ASSISTANT

PRESENCE: Time starts to move, slow at first, like a train moving off from a station. The new Planter, Robert Rose, sets off from Calcutta on a Bullock Cart. Somewhere in Nadia he stops, and the raiyats there touch his feet. He finds the sensation beautiful.

Out of the chorus, a white man emerges. ROBERT ROSE. He is 24.

Someone places marigold garlands round his neck; someone touches his feet.

PRESENCE: He is from near Worcester, in Worcestershire. Unlike Mr Lovegrove, a keen gardener, Mr Rose has no fixed hobbies. He will be one of only three Europeans in the district. He will leave behind him a scattering of letters, a bill from a racecourse near Jessore, and a few entries in the official logs of his concern.

MATTY GROVES

Night. A gathering, at the Planter's Bungalow.

Musicians play folk music.

Sitting on a solitary chair, listening appreciatively, is ROBERT ROSE, the garland still round his neck. He is intoxicated with his new world.

Around him are the villagers, including SADHU and KSHETROMANI, sitting on mats, singing. This is a performance in ROSE's honour.

CHORUS: Harvesting is in full swing
    The rain falls happily
    We plant crops, we harvest
    We make songs spontaneously

    ফসল কাটার ধুম নেগেছে
    (PHOSHOL KATAR DHUM NEGECHHEY)
    বিষ্টি এয়েলো সুকে
    (BISHTI EYELO SHUKEY)
    মোরা ফসল বুনি ফসল কাটি
    MORA PHOSHOL BUNI PHOSHOL KATI)
    গীত বান্দিছি মুকে
    GEET BANDICHI MUKEY)
    বিষ্টি এয়েলো সুকে।।
    (BISHTI EYELO SHUKEY)

    The soil has wakened up with raindrops
    Raptured in joy
    Leaves have been placed in our village
    Desiring for rice
    We're raptured in joy

    মাটি জেগেছে ফোটায় ফোটায়
    (MATI JAGECHEY PHOTAI PHOTAI)
    আহ্লাদে আটখানা
    (AHLADE AATKHANA)
    পাড়াগাঁয়ে পাত পইড়েছে
    (PARAGAYE PAAT POIRECHEY)
    ভাতের বাসনা
    (BHATER BASHNA)
    মোরা আহ্লাদে আটখানা।।
    (MORA AHLADE AATKHANA)

The song finishes.

ROSE: Wonderful! I'd like to say a few words.
    (*His hand on his heart*) First, I'd like to thank you for my welcome.
    I've found it...
    Magical.

I am in love with this paradise!

(*To GOPI*) Gopi, would you translate for me?

(*Explaining to everyone*) I'm sorry I do not yet know your language!

I know the old assistant was well-loved by you.

I hope you will love me like you loved him.

GOPI looks at ROSE, and translates:

GOPI: (*In Bangla*) Saheb welcomes you.

ROSE: When you deliver the harvest, expect fair treatment from my factory.

But times are changing.

The market is difficult.

The price of indigo is falling and the costs keep rising.

I have new instructions from Calcutta.

For the next crop we will issue new contracts at new rates.

We ask you to work harder, but for greater reward.

GOPI translates:

GOPI: (*In Bangla*) You must work harder. You must plant more nil.

ROSE: (*Smiling*) Does everyone understand?

The villagers are uncertain.

ROSE: I know it must be strange to have a new man here. Singing him your songs.

GOPI: Sir...

Mr Lovegrove Saheb.

He used to sing us English songs.

ROSE smiles

GOPI: Funny songs!

ROSE: Funny songs?

GOPI: Yes sir.

ROSE: I don't know many funny songs.

They look at him expectantly.

Let's see if I can remember something.

ROSE tries to conjure up a song.

ROSE: A holiday, a holiday and the first one of the year.[1]
Lord Darnell's wife came into church, the gospel for to hear.
And when the meeting it was done, she cast her eyes about,
And there she saw little Matty Groves, walking in the crowd.
'Come home with me, little Matty Groves, come home with me tonight.
Come home with me, little Matty Groves, and sleep with me till light.'

ROSE stops, uncertain of himself. The musicians begin to intuit the music. ROSE takes a drink from his hip flask.

ROSE: 'Oh, I can't come home, I won't come home and sleep with you tonight.
By the rings on your fingers I can tell, you are Lord Darnell's wife.'
'What if I am Lord Darnell's wife? Lord Darnell's not at home.
For he is out in the far cornfields, bringing the yearlings home.'

And now ROSE sees KSHETROMANI. He falls in love with her in an instant. He pretends she is Lady Darnell and offers her his hand.

ROSE: 'Come home with me, little Matty Groves, come home with me tonight.
Come home with me, little Matty Groves, and sleep with me till light.'

He smiles, but nobody knows what to do.

ROSE: Will someone else sing, now?

(*To KSHETROMANI*) Will you sing?

KSHETROMANI doesn't understand.

---

1 These lyrics derived from the traditional ballad 'Matty Groves' or 'The Ballad of Little Musgrave'.

GOPI: (*To KSHETROMANI, in Bangla*) He would like you to sing.

KSHETROMANI: (*In Bangla*) I'm not going to sing.

GOPI: You must sing.

SADHU: Excuse me, sir.

ROSE: Is there a problem?

GOPI: (*Discretely, to ROSE, of SADHU*) This is his wife, sir.

ROSE: Oh.

GOPI: In our /culture

ROSE: No—you don't need to explain to me!

(*He turns to SADHU*) I'm sorry.

'A thousand apologies'.
I'm just ignorant.
There was no harm intended on you.

SADHU looks at ROSE, but does not understand, quite yet.
But KSHETROMANI understands. She sees ROSE.

ROSE: (*To SADHU*) What's your name?

SADHU: Sadhu Charan.

ROSE: (*Shaking his hand*) I'm please to meet you, Sadhu Charan.

SADHU holds ROSE's hand. He inclines his head.

Are you going to bring me your indigo, Sadhu Charan?

And what does SADHU see in ROSE's smile, in this moment?

You're cutting it tomorrow?

And does ROSE see that KSHETROMANI knows what ROSE is going to do?
And does this unsettle him?

ROSE: Don't worry, I'll give you a good rate! I'll give a good rate to all true friends of the concern!

And SADHU sees it. He turns away, afraid.

And ROSE sees that SADHU knows what is inside him?

Do not worry! It's all alright! It's all alright! I'll remember you, Sadhu Charan.

AN OLD FRIEND

By SADHU's house. SADHU and KSHETROMANI work in their field.

NABINA Madhab enters, an intellectual of the Bengal renaissance, in strikingly modern hair and clothing.

NABINA: Hey! Brother!

SADHU stares at her.

NABINA: (*conducting a joke*) I am lost, brother!

SADHU: Where are you going?

NABINA looks at SADHU, hoping he gets the joke.

NABINA: Kanaipur.

SADHU: Follow the river and you'll get to the path.

NABINA: Sadhu, brother——do you not recognise me? Have I changed so much?

SADHU: Nabina sister?

NABINA: The same!

SADHU: I did not recognise you!

NABINA: My hair.

SADHU: And your dress!
Kshetromani, this is Nabina, she is the Landlord's daughter. Living in Calcutta.

NABINA: (*Of KSHETROMANI*) And who is this?

SADHU: This is my wife!

KSHETROMANI makes to touch NABINA's feet, but NABINA moves away.

NABINA: No no, please. The honour is all mine.

How long since the wedding?

SADHU: Two months.

NABINA: And I was not invited?

SADHU: We invited you... Perhaps the message did not reach you in Calcutta?

Pause.

NABINA: I heard that Mr Lovegrove passed.

SADHU: Yes.

NABINA: And the new man? Rose. How is he?

SADHU: We do not know enough of him.

NABINA: Something is changing, in the division. In Swarpur there have been people gone missing.
Beatings, false imprisonment. They are forcing men to take advances. Two rupees a bundle.

KSHETROMANI: Two rupees!

SADHU: Not possible.

NABINA: Two rupees, yes.

SADHU: Swarpur is far.

NABINA: Far, yes. But Swarpur is part of Rose's Concern. Can you tell me brother, have there been yet any prosecutions under the new law?

SADHU: What new law?

NABINA: (*Passionately*) They make it a criminal offence to break an indigo contract!
First they force the contract—then say we cannot break it.
And cannot protest against the contracts!
They bring men to the courts on false and unjust charges!

Police are against us.
In Meherpur, a man took his life himself because he could not
fight the courts. What could he do?
When the Magistrate is against us?
What can we do
When the Planters are against us?

SADHU: I hope you can resolve it all quickly

NABINA: The time will come when we will play our own part. Here.
(*To KSHETROMANI, of SADHU*) I remember this one.

We used to be friends, despite the difference in our birth. We
used to play in the rapids. Do you remember? Jumping off the
bank like a wild thing.
He used to fight, too.

SADHU: I did not fight.

NABINA: There was a time you took on Binoy from Ratanbari.
Laid him out cold when he tried to threaten us. Sadhu was our
protector!

SADHU: That was a long time ago.

KSHETROMANI looks at SADHU.

NABINA: There was once a time when I thought it was you who'd
be the leader.

SADHU: Me?

NABINA: I never considered it an option for me on account of
my sex. But these last years have changed me. A dark time is
coming. Chaos.
But we are waking up. These people must be stopped, don't you
think, brother?

SADHU: I do not know.

NABINA: (*To KSHETROMANI*) What do you think, Sister?

KSHETROMANI: I do not think.

NABINA: Then we must school you.

KSHETROMANI: No.

NABINA: In Calcutta there are many ladies in the fight.

KSHETROMANI: What is there that can be done? (*Angrily*) Against these people? I do not think there is anything that you can do.

NABINA: I have written in the English newspapers.

KSHETROMANI: What good are newspapers?

SADHU: (*Gently*) Kshetromani.

KSHETROMANI: You babus have written in newspapers for years.

SADHU: (*Raising his voice a little*) Hey!

KSHETROMANI: Writing in newspapers achieves nothing.

NABINA realises she cannot match KSHETROMANI's anger.

NABINA: I miss this. I miss this, so much. This golden land.
(*To KSHETROMANI*) It was a pleasure, to meet you.
And you, brother, I am so happy to renew our acquaintance.
Please, if I can be of any assistance, you can find me at the Zamindary.

NABINA exits.

KSHETROMANI: She is a fool.

SADHU: You cannot speak to her like that.

KSHETROMANI: Are you too simple to understand?
It is happening again?

SADHU: Be at peace, my love.
What can happen?
Today we deliver ten first-grade bundles.
Mr Lovegrove always said our crop was district best.
Let's be happy today.

KSHETROMANI: You're right. I'm sorry.

She touches his face. There is some love here.

And there will be a few moments more where everything can still be alright, when
SADHU can dance, and even KSHETROMANI can dance.

The community joins them.

CHORUS: The leaves of the Neel plant are green
But a forest is greener
The green of the forest
Lives in my heart
To whom I surrender my life

নীল গাছের পাতা সবুজ
(NEEL GACHER PATA SHOBUJ)
আরও সবুজ বন
(AARO SHOBUJ BON)
বনের সবুজ মনে বাঁচে
(BONER SHOBUJ MONE BACHEY)
জীবন সমর্পণ
(JIBON SHOMORPON)

Burns like blue, my anxious soul
Sings the song of the end of the harvest
In my dream, I see an elated firefly night
About to emerge

নীল দহন মন উচাটন
(NEEL DOHON MON UCHATON)
গাই ফসল শেষের গীত
(GAAI PHOSHOL SHESHER GEET)
স্বপ্নে দেকি ঐ জাগিছে
(SHOPNEY DEKI OI JAGICHEY)
জোনাক জ্বলা নিশীথ
(JONAK JOLA NISHITH)

On a fortunate day
Dipped in blue of the Neel tree
On a Cuckoo calling morning
Good days will surely come back
Let the good days come back.
Let them come back.

নীল গাছের রঙে নীলা
(NEEL GACHHER RONGEY NEELA)
পয়মন্ত দিনে
(POYMONTO DINEY)
কোকিল ডাকা ভোরে
(KOKIL DAKA BHOREY)
সুদিন আসবি ফিরে
(SHUDIN ASHBI PHIREY)
ফের আসবি সুদিন ফিরে
(PHER SHUDIN ASHBI PHIREY)
ফের আসুক সুদিন ফিরে।।
(PHER ASHUK SHUDIN PHIREY)

ACT TWO – THE FACTORY

I CAN SEE IT EVERYWHERE

The present day. A denim factory. Huge dyeing vats, in which a thousand threads of cotton are dyed—ready to be woven into denim.

RUPA works there.

PRESENCE: Her name is Rupa.
She works shifts in the new factory.
She receives $115 dollars a month.
It is something. It is better than it used to be.

The PRESENCE questions her.

PRESENCE: What are you making?

RUPA: I am dying the thread.

PRESENCE: What will the thread become?

RUPA: The thread will become denim.

PRESENCE: Is the work dangerous?

RUPA: I am skilled with it.

PRESENCE: Does it harm your hands?

RUPA: They supply gloves.

PRESENCE: And masks?

RUPA: They supply masks, yes, but I do not wear them.

PRESENCE: Why not?

She shrugs.

Do they treat you well?

RUPA: It's hard. But they are making efforts.

Something spews out of a pipe, into the river, a huge gush of effluence.

PRESENCE: The factory was not built on deep foundations. The dyeing process uses huge amounts of water.

Something spews out of the pipe.

The effluence from the dye flows straight into the river?

RUPA: (*Scolding him*) All your questions are about this factory!

PRESENCE: Of course.

RUPA: All you are interested in is 'are you exploited?', 'Is the factory bad?'

PRESENCE: What else would I ask about?

RUPA: What about me?
Are you not interested in me?

PRESENCE: Are you depressed?

RUPA: No, I am not depressed.

PRESENCE: How do you feel about this place?

RUPA: Feel? I am interested in it. I think about it.

PRESENCE: What do you think about?

RUPA: I think about the dyeing process. I think we could improve it. I think about how we could strengthen the depth of colour.

The PRESENCE does not know what to do with this.

PRESENCE: I think you are a leader.

RUPA: Me? I am not a leader.

MINA, RUPA's friend, enters.

They smile at each other.

MINA takes RUPA's hand.

RUPA: Are you OK?

MINA: Yes.

A male supervisor enters, and grins at MINA. MINA tries to avoid his gaze.
RUPA gives him evils. He leaves.

RUPA: (*Of the supervisor*) Has he done something?

MINA: He just likes to play games.

RUPA: More than games.

MINA: He likes to humiliate me.

RUPA: I will break his balls.

MINA: He's OK, really.

RUPA: No.

MINA: He's so stressed.
We're so behind this month.

RUPA: Shall we walk home together?

MINA: Tonight I have a late shift.

RUPA: You are too tired.

MINA:(*Shaking her head*) I'm OK.

RUPA: And studying on top of this.

MINA: I'm not studying.
I gave it up.

RUPA: Why?

MINA: What's the point?
I'm not smart like you.

RUPA: No, no...

MINA has a panic attack.

MINA: I'm not...
I'm not...
I'm nothing...
I'm nothing.
I'm just shit.

RUPA: It's OK. It's OK.

MINA nearly collapses.

Here, sit down. Feeling faint?

She sits MINA down.

You'll be OK.

MINA: The blood.
It's like all the blood in my head is rushing away.
Like I'm shrinking.

Pause.

RUPA gives MINA water.

MINA: I can't do this anymore.
I owe so much money.
I can't afford to pay it back.
I can see it everywhere.

RUPA: What is it?

MINA: It's coming out of here.

RUPA: What, Mina?

MINA: The giant.

RUPA: The giant?

MINA: The Daitya.

MINA grasps RUPA'S hand.

You mustn't let it take you, Rupa.
You have something.
I know you have something.

THE NILKUTHI

The PRESENCE introduces us to the indigo factory.

PRESENCE: The indigo factory.
  The Nilkuthi.
  Farmers transport bundles
  of Indigofera Tinctoria to the factory.
  First the plant is steeped in great tanks of water. The water
  turns a greeny yellow white.
  Then, it is released into the lower tank, where eight men churn
  the liquid, binding the indigo with oxygen
  Turning the water blue.
  This liquid is then siphoned, dried into a paste, and then pressed
  into cakes, ready for export. It is a miraculous transformation.
  The delivery of the indigo,
  traditionally a great moment in the life of the community! A day
  of joy!

THE FACTORY

*SADHU is at the indigo factory —the 'Nilkuthi'. He has brought many huge
bundles of indigo plant —Indigofera Tinctoria. GOPI is there, with a huge chain,
that he places round the indigo in order to measure it. Beside him, on a table is his
large accounts ledger.*

SADHU: (*Pleading*) Gopi-uncle.

GOPI: Sorry, Sadhu.

SADHU: This is not the price.

GOPI: Unfortunately, the price has fallen!

SADHU: Three rupees per bundle.

GOPI: No one will pay three rupees per bundle, not in Bengal.

SADHU: It was the rate agreed with Lovegrove Saheb.

GOPI: I do not remember.

SADHU: You were there! (*Increasingly panicked*) We agreed.

GOPI: There is no contract in my file.

SADHU: You were there.

GOPI: Alas, I have no record.

SADHU: Uncle!

GOPI examines the bundle.

GOPI: SADHU, how can I give you three rupees for this?
The quality is not first rate.

SADHU: Saheb said my crop is the best in the district.

GOPI: We are coming to realise that Saheb was not an expert.
You used to stuff the bundle with paddy. Your bundles
weakened our blue. Last time you delivered, the crop was
useless. Lovegrove didn't say a word to spare your feelings.

SADHU: Uncle.

GOPI: Don't 'uncle' me. Your crop is shit. I'm sorry, Sadhu.

SADHU: But he paid me, 30 rupees.

GOPI: In advance of ten first-grade bundles.

SADHU: But if you record two rupees for the bundle, and ten
bundles.

GOPI: Yes.

SADHU: I must give you money back.

GOPI: Yes.

SADHU: How much?

GOPI: Ten rupees only.

SADHU: (*Panicking*) Ten rupees! How can I give you ten rupees?

GOPI: Why should we lose out, for your idleness? These will not
produce the indigo we need.

SADHU: Sir, please!

GOPI: What can I do?

SADHU: Three rupees for a bundle!

GOPI: Two rupees.

SADHU: I cannot pay you ten rupees!
That is three months...
I have other payments to make!

GOPI: What other payments?

SADHU: I have other loans. The wedding.

GOPI: You foolish child.

SADHU tries to work it through in his head but can't —this is a disaster.

GOPI: (*A gentle hand on SADHU*) You've got to understand, son.

SADHU cries out.

SADHU: I cannot!

ROSE appears.

ROSE: What's happening?

GOPI: Sir!

ROSE: There is some dispute?

GOPI: Yes, sir.

ROSE: Surely we can settle it like friends? Yes?

(*ROSE recognises SADHU*) I recognise him. This man is a friend of the concern.

GOPI: He will not accept the price.

ROSE: (*To SADHU*) The price we pay is the price paid all over Bengal.

GOPI: He will be in shortfall.

ROSE: He cannot repay his advance?

GOPI: No sir.

SADHU: I agreed price with Lovegrove Saheb.

ROSE: How much?

SADHU: Three rupees

ROSE: (*To GOPI*) How much will he be in shortfall?

GOPI: Ten rupees

ROSE nods his head wisely, and deliberates.

ROSE: (*Sympathetically, to SADHU*) I can see the problem, of course I can.
But the situation is: Mr Lovegrove Saheb—and I don't want to speak ill of a loved and respected man—was not authorised to pay that.
The price was always two rupees.

Pause.

ROSE experiences the pleasure in taking a hard line.

That's what we've been paying across the country, for bundles of this quality.

SADHU: The quality is good.

ROSE: I'm afraid, not good enough.

SADHU: My indigo is district best.

ROSE examines it. It's like he fancies himself a connoisseur.

ROSE: No, you are mistaken. This is of a medium grade.

SADHU: Sir.

ROSE: I am expert in assessing the leaves.

SADHU: Why do you do this?

ROSE: It's alright, friend.

SADHU: What have I done to you?

ROSE: You don't understand.

SADHU: I will return the advance.

GOPI: You cannot return the advance.

SADHU: I will return it

ROSE: It is against the law to break an indigo contract.

Pause.

SADHU turns to GOPI in bewilderment.

GOPI: You made a contract with us to supply 30 rupees worth of
indigo.
If you break the contract you could serve six months in prison.
You cannot return it, Sadhu, also because you have spent it.

Pause.

ROSE: Look, I can't write off the ten rupees, it isn't worth my
job, but what I can do for you...
What I will do, is let you off five rupees, and lend you five,
with low interest.
How does that sound? Do you think that's fair?
And when we talk about the new crop, we'll come to it with a
fresh mind.
That sounds fair, doesn't it?

ROSE takes SADHU's silence as an acceptance of terms.

ROSE: I wish to live up to Mr Lovegrove Saheb.

*He locks eyes with SADHU and namastes, and SADHU knows there is
something going wrong with ROBERT ROSE.*

CHORUS: The giant is coming. The Daitya!
Don't you hear it? The Daitya!
Can't you hear the footsteps all around?
The indigo giant is coming!

ঐ আসে রাক্ষুসে। দানব, দানব!
(OI ASHEY RAKKHUSHEY, DANOB, DANOB!)
শুনতে কি পাও না? দানব দানব!
(SHUNTEY KI PAU NA? DANOB, DANOB!)
পাও না কি শুনতে পায়ের আওয়াজ চারিপাশে?
(PAU NA KI SHUNTEY PAYER AOWAJ CHARPASHEY?)
নীল দানব ছায়া ঐ আসে, ঐ আসে!
(NEEL DANOB CHHAYA OI ASHEY OI ASHEY)

INFINITY

ROSE, by an indigo vat. There is a washing-line hanging between pillars. Wearing leather gloves, he dips a length of white cotton into the vat. He pulls it out. It is yellowy-green. He holds it up, fascinated.

He dips the cloth in the vat once again, watching the strange colour. He assesses the fabric.

He pegs the fabric onto the washing line. He watches its strange colour. Then he sees someone pass across the way.

ROSE: (*Calling out*) Hello!
Hello!
Sister!
You can come out.

KSHETROMANI enters, guardedly.

(*Practising his Bangla*) Ashun?

She stares at him.

It's alright.

Pause.

He approaches her, and she takes a step back.

It's alright.
There is no trouble.
Please sit.

She does not sit.

Boshun. Is that right?
My Bengali—I've been trying to learn!
I have been messing about with a vat, do you want to see? Do you want to see? I'm wondering if this will become a hobby!

Apni dekhte
Was that right?

KSHETROMANI: 'Apni' na—'Tumi'.

ROSE: But why should I not use the respectful form of address for you?
You are not my servant.
In my country we all considered equal.
(*Of the dyeing*) Would you like to see?
Would you show me?

He takes off his gloves and offers them to her.

ROSE: Go on - take them.
Put them on.

KSHETROMANI: (*Smiling, shaking her head*) Na.

ROSE: Go on, put them on. If you like.

She puts them on. She feels the heat left by his hands. She looks at him, uncertain, the gloves so big.

ROSE: That's wonderful!

He takes another length of white cotton, and gives it to her. She holds it.

ROSE: Lancashire cotton!

You can dip it in the vat. If you like.

He gestures the vat.

Would you like to dip it in the vat?

Pause.

She looks up at him.

Go on.

Pause.

She dips the cotton in the vat. She churns it around a bit. She pulls it out, greeny-yellow. She is fascinated with the colour.

Look at that!
It's like magic—the way it turns to blue.

She smiles at him.

He looks at it in wonder.

(*Of the cotton*) Dip it in again.

She dips it in again. She tries to pull it out, but he puts his hand in the vat in order to keep the cotton in longer.

No, keep it in longer.

She gasps, realising that his bare hand is in the dye. He pulls his hand out. It is greenish yellow.

I suppose I'll have to have a dyed hand!

She steps back, horrified.

I think you have a very fine soul. Like silk.
I love how distant you are from me.
But then, even in England, women are distant. I don't know what it is.

Pause.

He turns to look at the dyed fabric, which is already oxidizing, and turning blue. He points to the cotton.

Can you see the transformation?
What is it, that causes this change? From yellow-green to indigo?
It's in the breeze. In the air.
Do you love your husband? Do you love?
On most days I feel nothing, but something in the breeze has brought me this transformation.

He reaches out again to touch her cheek and she takes a step back.

ROSE looks at his hand and sees that it is turning blue.

My hand is turning blue.

ROSE raises his hand to her cheek, slowly. She watches it approach her face, and turns away.

I feel like I'm getting it wrong the whole time.
But... you see me.

They breathe for a moment.

ROSE produces a handkerchief.

Inside is something wrapped in wax paper: bright indigo, a broken cake of it looks like gemstones.

ROSE: Take it.

KSHETROMANI: No, I cannot.

ROSE: Please.

KSHETROMANI: How many bighas of land, how many bundles, to make this amount?

ROSE: Are you so mean and small, to count?
Just place it in your hand, for a moment.

I sense—that you were not born to work fields.
You were once part of greatness.
You, your family, were bigger than this.
That is where you must go again.

ROSE holds the indigo near her. She feels its magical properties.

See how deep it is. See how much you want it.
When I look at indigo, I see oceans.
I see the sky on a starlit night.
Listen to it.

He puts it close to KSHETROMANI's ear.

Can you hear it?
Indigo sings a song that goes on forever.
It wants you.
Take it and you will not be small any more.

KSHETROMANI does not take it.

SADHU enters.

He sees ROSE and KSHETROMANI, together.

He makes himself known.

KSHETROMANI pulls away from ROSE.

ROSE: (*To SADHU*) It's alright, friend. There's no problem.
She was only walking by.

And something strikes at SADHU's heart.

ROSE goes over to shake SADHU's hand, but SADHU does not shake. Then SADHU sees ROSE has a blue hand!

ROSE: (*trying to make SADHU smile*) Oh yes! I am blue!
Like Krishna!
Our Lord Protector!
Don't look so worried.

All will be well.
I'll come round tomorrow with my book.
About the new advance.
I'll give you a better rate!
Better than last time

I must wash my hand!

ROSE exits.

KSHETROMANI: It was nothing.

SADHU tries to breathe.

KSHETROMANI: He called me to look—it was nothing.

He struggles to breathe.

KSHETROMANI: What is it?

SADHU: It doesn't matter.

KSHETROMANI: Your breathing.

SADHU controls his breathing.

SADHU: There's no problem.

KSHETROMANI: Did something happen at the factory?

SADHU: No.

KSHETROMANI: The advance has been fulfilled?

SADHU: Yes.

KSHETROMANI: We will need money soon.

SADHU: It's no problem.

KSHETROMANI: You are certain nothing happened?

SADHU: (*Raising his voice a little*) Why do you keep asking this?
I am sorry.

KSHETROMANI: Rose. He did nothing. He meant nothing.

He struggles to breathe.

She puts a gentle hand on his cheek.

Your breathing, again...
Tell me what it is.

SADHU: It's nothing.

KSHETROMANI: You must tell me.

SADHU: No.

KSHETROMANI: I know the look in your eyes.
It is a look I have seen before.
When men lie to themselves.
What happened at the kuthi?
How much do we owe them?

SADHU: We do not owe them.

KSHETROMANI: Swear to me.

SADHU: Do not doubt me.

KSHETROMANI: Swear

Angrily, he raises his hand.

SADHU: Hey.

KSHETROMANI: *(Of his violence)* What did you just do?

He lowers his hand and his head in shame.

What did you just do?

Pause.

He exits.

KSHETROMANI, upset.

The PRESENCE enters.

KSHETROMANI doesn't want The PRESENCE there either.

PRESENCE: He raised his hand?
Has he ever done that before?

Pause.

KSHETROMANI: No. He is kind.
I don't know what is taking him over.
But I have seen it before.

PRESENCE: Your father?

KSHETROMANI: He brought our family to the dust.

PRESENCE: Your father was in debt?

KSHETROMANI: I will not talk of it.

PRESENCE: Every farmer in Kanaipur owes money.

KSHETROMANI: Not Sadhu.

PRESENCE: He has promised you?

KSHETROMANI: He had a special rate.

PRESENCE: Even so, you may wish to consider
That you have a choice of actions.
Rose... You have seen the way he looks at you.

KSHETROMANI: I would not do that.

PRESENCE: I am not arguing for it.
But know: you will be greater than this.
Look at your clothes.
These modest clothes.
These clothes that say 'I do not want anything more'
I only want you to know: you have a choice of action.
Because the Indigo Giant is coming.

CHORUS:
The Daitya!
Don't you hear it? The Daitya!
Can't you hear the footsteps all around!
The Indigo Giant is coming.

রাক্ষুসে!
(RAKKHUSHEY!)
শুনতে কি পাও না? দানব দানব!
(SHUNTEY KI PAU NA? DANOB, DANOB!)
পাও না কি শুনতে পায়ের আওয়াজ চারিপাশে?
(PAU NA KI SHUNTEY PAYER AOWAJ CHARPASHEY?)
নীল দানব ছায়া ঐ আসে, ঐ আসে!
(NEEL DANOB CHHAYA OI ASHEY OI ASHEY)

INDIGO IN THE HEAD

SADHU's hut.

GOPI: Hoy SADHU Charan!

SADHU: Yes, GOPI uncle!

GOPI saunters onto the porch with his account ledger and a large bag of seed.

GOPI: You have an important visitor. Hoy!

ROSE enters. KSHETROMANI covers her face, and shrinks to the periphery. ROSE ostentatiously takes his shoes off, and offers greetings.

ROSE: Namaste!
So, this is your home?
Thank you, for allowing me to be here

SADHU: (*To KSHETROMANI*) What can we offer him?

GOPI: (*To ROSE*) Would you like anything to eat?

ROSE: I do not wish to burden them.

KSHETROMANI: (*To SADHU, in Bangla*) We do not have anything to give. .

SADHU: (*To KSHETROMANI, in Bangla*) You can find some sweets? Maybe he will not eat them?

KSHETROMANI goes off. ROSE addresses SADHU.

ROSE: Even as we wave a farewell to the last crop, we turn to the next.
Her majesty's navy has commissioned 100,000 new uniforms.
I have instructions from my company to increase the production of indigo.
Do you understand?

GOPI: (*In Bangla*) This time you will have to produce more.

SADHU: (*Dismayed*) More? How much more?

KSHETROMANI comes in with a little banana leaf with sweets on it.

ROSE: Oh! You didn't have to go to any trouble!

He does not take the sweets.

ROSE: Please—you eat them!

SADHU: (*To GOPI, in Bangla*) How much does he want?

ROSE: This year we would like you will plant 20 bighas of your fields with indigo.

SADHU: What?

GOPI: (*In Bangla*) This year you will plant 20 bighas of land with indigo.

Pause.

SADHU looks at the bag with horror. GOPI places his account ledger on a table in expectation of SADHU signing.

GOPI: (*in Bangla*) Torap next door has already agreed to 20 bighas. Mr Lal has agreed to 30.

KSHETROMANI: (*In Bangla*) No.

GOPI: (*In Bangla*) Take the seed.
Take the seed, Sadhu.
Do not worry, you will still have land for rice.

ROSE puts his hand in the seed sack, takes out a handful, offers it to SADHU.

ROSE: I will give you a good rate.

GOPI: (*In Bangla*) He will give you a good rate.

KSHETROMANI: (*In Bangla*) No.

SADHU begins to edge away.

ROSE: If the crop is good, I will pay you a good rate.

SADHU: How much?

ROSE: Better than two.

SADHU: Saheb

Pause.

GOPI looks at ROSE.

ROSE: I will give you a good deal!

SADHU: What deal? Advance?

ROSE picks up the sack.

ROSE: In advance, I will give you... 50 rupees, for 20 bighas.

SADHU: I cannot!

ROSE: And I will cancel your debt to me.

GOPI: (*In Bangla*) He will cancel your debt

KSHETROMANI: (*In Bangla*) His debt?
You told me there was no debt.

SADHU turns away, ashamed.

(*Bangla*) What debt?

ROSE, smiling, takes SADHU's hand, and pours a handful of seed into it.

ROSE: Come, I do not wish to beg you.

SADHU puts the seed back into the bag.

ROSE: You won't plant my indigo?

SADHU: I cannot plant it.
    If I plant 20 bighas, I cannot plant rice.
    Indigo takes three times the work as rice.
    If I plant indigo, we will not eat.
    We will die.

SADHU goes to ROSE's feet, and touches them. ROSE stops.

He experiences a strange feeling.

ROSE looks around the room. He sees the clay figures, in their variety.

ROSE: (*Of the clay figures*) I have seen clay figures like these before.
    Did you make them?

GOPI: His father.

ROSE: Is he...

GOPI: He died, sir.

ROSE: Oh, I'm sorry.
    There are some like these in the Bungalow. The previous
    assistant. He seemed to have collected them.

ROSE takes up two of the figures.

    Can you explain them to me?
    Who is this, and who is this?

GOPI: (*Explaining the figures*) This is a merchant, and this is a barber.

ROSE: Will you tell me about it. I mean, I don't understand...
    Who is the bigger man, and who is the lesser?

SADHU shows him.

And now ROSE has a white man and a Bengal raiyat.

ROSE: And look what else I have found – a white man, and a
    black man.
    Who is higher and who is lower?

What is the correct order of things?

Now he produces statues of Shiva and Krishna.

And how about these?
Shiva? Destroyer?
And Krishna?
Protector?

Pause.

SADHU closes his eyes.

Pause.

ROSE takes one of the sweets. He chews it appreciatively.

ROSE: (*Of the sweet*) This is good. Thank you.
May I ask of you again—will you take the advance?

SADHU: No sir.

KSHETROMANI kneels and touches ROSE's feet. ROSE experiences the supplication and feels ashamed. He extricates himself.

ROSE: So—we must take our leave of you. You have laid out your position and I have laid out mine. We will both have to give it some thought.

Pause.

(*To KSHETROMANI*) You do not need to kneel to me.

ROSE exits.

GOPI follows him, though they leave the bag of seed.

KSHETROMANI: SADHU?

SADHU: You see? He will not force us.

KSHETROMANI: He has left the seed.
How much debt are we in?

SADHU: We will manage it.

KSHETROMANI:
How much?

He goes to her. She puts her hands up to make him keep his distance.

KSHETROMANI: Can you not feel it coming?

SADHU: What?

KSHETROMANI: In your blood, in your breathing. Fingers round your heart.

SADHU: (*Of a deity*) He will protect us.

KSHETROMANI: Who?

Pause.

SADHU indicates some blessed presence.

Pause.

He goes to her.

SADHU: Please.

He goes to touch her.

My love for you is strong.

KSHETROMANI: That will not help!

She puts her hand on her belly.

And now ROSE has returned. He carries a journal.

ROSE: I forgot to say. I just found this lying around the Bungalow. Lovegrove Saheb's journal! Did you know he wrote a journal? I have been reading it! He mentions your father, specifically. Your father was Mr Ray Charan, was it not? Do you read English?

What does Mr Lovegrove call him? Let me try to find the precise line...

'Ray Charan is a dull-headed fool, who comes to nuisance me at night. Try as I might to indicate I am tired, he persists in hovering on the edge of the verandah with that straggly little wretch of a boy, his son.'

Pause.

SADHU: Can I see?

ROSE: Can you read English?

SADHU: No.

ROSE: No, you cannot read it, so I cannot show you the line.
I am sick of living up to Lovegrove. I have tried, so hard to feel it, but I do not believe he was possible.
The white Bengali.
The missionary planter.
The man who set up a school for the little children.
What I want to know is...
Who did he fuck over?
Who did he fuck?
Did he fuck you?
And who did he kill?
Because I have been doing very careful calculations.
And I have established you cannot grow indigo with free men.

Will you plant me 20 bighas of indigo, Sadhu Charan?

SADHU: No.

ROSE: Will you plant my seed?

SADHU: I will not plant it, sir.

KSHETROMANI: Sadhu.

ROSE: Do you love your wife?
You can't look after her.
At my house, she would be happy.
I wouldn't beat her.

SADHU: I do not beat her.

ROSE: (*To Kshetromoni*) He does not beat you?

SADHU: No!

ROSE: You will, one day. And then she will come to me.

SADHU: (*Furious*) Why do you say these things to me?

ROSE: That's good.

SADHU roars with anger.

ROSE: That's where I want you.
You will take my advance, or I'll lock you in the go-down.
Even if you have to lose everything you will take it, and
everyone will say 'look, Sadhu Charan has taken the advance,
after all'.
Come here.

SADHU does not move.

Come here, I'm not going to hurt you.

SADHU wavers.

I want to show you what I will do.

*SADHU goes over to him, slowly. ROSE kneels down in the mud. He looks up
at SADHU, then scoops up some of the mud in one hand. Slowly, he rises to his
feet.*

ROSE: It's alright.

*ROSE smears the mud over SADHU's head, until the top of his head is covered
in mud.*

Then ROSE takes some seeds from the bag.

ROSE: Do you know what I'm going to do?

ROSE begins to put seeds into the clay on SADHU's head.

ROSE: I will plant indigo in your head.

ROSE plants indigo in SADHU's head.

SADHU crumbles onto the floor. He has a crown of clay on his head.

There is a silence.

Then there is a sound, a muffled far-off sound, a boom, like cannon-fire, or giant's footsteps. SADHU keeps his eyes closed. He tries to battle whatever is there, whatever is happening to him.

ACT THREE - THE GO-DOWN

THE BUYER

The present day. The garments factory. RUPA in the factory. She is now in an enclosed room—as cell-like as SADHU's go-down.

SUPERVISOR: The Buyer is coming.
He wants to interview you.

RUPA: Why?
Why should I see him?

SUPERVISOR: He is worried about what happened to Mina.
If he asks about her, say you do not know anything.
If he takes his business elsewhere, we'll be finished.

JEREMY, head of sustainability at a large clothing brand, enters. RUPA goes to touch his feet, but JEREMY waves her away.

JEREMY: Please don't.

RUPA looks up at him. She moves back.

I don't want those kind of relations.

The pipe spews filth into the river.

JEREMY: (*To SUPERVISOR*) And it goes straight in?

SUPERVISOR: We are working on the discharge.

JEREMY: Yes, but...

SUPERVISOR: This is a denim dyeing factory, sir.

JEREMY: Yes.

SUPERVISOR: Water is blue, sir.

JEREMY looks at him with contempt.

JEREMY: (*To SUPERVISOR*) You can leave us now.

SUPERVISOR: (*Suspicious*) Sir?

JEREMY: Look, I should just say again, I'm not here to check up on anyone. As you know, my customers want to know that we're producing this clothing ethically.
And in particular, we're really keen that, obviously, mental health is good, that they're getting what they need in order to do their jobs.
Would I be able to talk to this woman alone?

SUPERVISOR: Alone, sir?

JEREMY: Yes.

The supervisor stares at RUPA.

SUPERVISOR: No problem.

The SUPERVISOR leaves JEREMY and RUPA.

JEREMY ushers her to a seat.

JEREMY: Please sit.

She sits. He sits.

I see you're wearing your gloves?

RUPA: Yes sir.

JEREMY: But not your facemask?

RUPA: No sir.

JEREMY: Did they give you one?

RUPA: I do not like to wear it.

JEREMY: I see. Is it uncomfortable? We could try another brand.

RUPA: I don't know, sir.

JEREMY writes something down in his book.

JEREMY: Look, I'm wearing a pair of our jeans now. London Midnight. They have an amazing colour, a colour that seems to get more subtle with every wash.

Sometimes I look at my legs. I mean, with these jeans on, and I stare at them. These legs! We rely on you to create these legs. This look.

You are part of our team. The market for our garments is going to grow in the next five years. We want to take you with us. Do you understand?

The PRESENCE intervenes, speaking only to RUPA.

PRESENCE: There are things you should tell him.
Things about the process, that only you know
About how to deepen the colour
How to make it last.
How to reduce gallons of water.
There are people growing natural indigo again.

RUPA: (*To The PRESENCE*) That isn't what he wants to hear.

PRESENCE: He wants to listen to you.

RUPA: No.

JEREMY: I was so sorry to hear about your colleague. Mina Huq.

RUPA turns away.

I know you probably don't want to talk about that. But I want to know how can we avoid that happening again?
Would you like to say anything?

RUPA shakes her head, closes her eyes. Manages herself.

PRESENCE: (*To her alone*) Do not hold it back.

RUPA: I can't say anything.

PRESENCE: He wants to hear it.

RUPA: He doesn't want to hear it.

PRESENCE: He is asking you.

RUPA: When they found Mina we closed for half a day while they got her body down. We were late for ten orders.

Pause. This is not what she wanted to say.

JEREMY: Why did she do it?

RUPA: Do you think there is an easy answer?

JEREMY: I understand she was in debt.
(*To RUPA*) You OK?
I know, it's hard, isn't it? We were so sad, in the London office, when we heard.
I'm sorry to put it this way—but if people are committing suicide here, we can't buy from you. Our customers will think we are mistreating our workers.
If something is wrong, we need to know.

RUPA: I do not know what to say.

JEREMY: Look, if you ever need to contact me, in person, you can get me on WhatsApp.

He gives her his card. She takes it. JEREMY gets up, and touches RUPA on the arm again, in a collegiate way.

JEREMY: Anyway, I need to go. Thank you so much, Rupa.

JEREMY leaves.

THE SUPERVISOR enters.

SUPERVISOR: Well?

She says nothing.

SUPERVISOR: What did you say to him?

RUPA: Nothing.

SUPERVISOR: What did you say to him?

RUPA: I said nothing!

SUPERVISOR: Did he ask about Mina?

RUPA: (*An outburst*) There is something not right here!

SUPERVISOR: What?

RUPA: In this cement, in this place.

SUPERVISOR: The engineer has come.

RUPA: I'm not talking about the crack.

SUPERVISOR: What are you talking about? We are doing
everything, this is a good factory.

RUPA: I know.

SUPERVISOR: I am sick of this Union shit. We do <u>everything</u>
for you in this factory.
And you want to be victim all the time.

SUPERVISOR gets his phone.

Look at my phone: I can stream Netflix.
Look at my watch!
I have dollars.
I will not live in poverty anymore.
You tell me I should not come to this factory.
Of course, I'll come
And take this money.
Maybe it will never come again.

RUPA: I know.

SUPERVISOR: Maybe this is our only chance... We have to take it.

RUPA: Yes.

SUPERVISOR: You have gloves.
And a facemask.
And $115 a month.
Your father could not dream of $115.

RUPA: No.

SUPERVISOR: Your father is ruined now. With Mina... I didn't do anything.

RUPA: I know.

SUPERVISOR: It wasn't my fault!

RUPA: I know.

SUPERVISOR: I didn't hurt her. I was just so stressed and I teased her.
And she was in debt.

RUPA: I know.

SUPERVISOR exits.

Pause.

The PRESENCE comes to her.

RUPA: I see her everywhere.

Suddenly, it is night, and we see that RUPA can see a figure, hanging from a beam.

They are dripping like wet denim, hung out to dry.

RUPA: I can see it everywhere.

PRESENCE: What is it?

RUPA: It's coming out of here.
It's everywhere, it's in the soil.
A week ago, I was walking home when I saw a face in the paddy. A face under water and mud.
That pale white face, almost blue, like a dead thing. Its eyes closed.
I covered it in mud and I walked away.
The next day I returned to the fields it had emerged again.
Just a white face. I went closer.
I felt the chill.

I felt a sickness.
Its eyes opened. I screamed.
Then, out of the mud ripped its arm
And clutched me.
I screamed with the terror.
I screamed because I knew who this was.
I'd seen him before, lifetimes ago.
A giant.

Do you ever feel that there is something inside you, something very old, that will come out one day? That will rise out of the earth?

PRESENCE: Don't you remember what happened here?

RUPA: I do not remember.

PRESENCE: Don't you remember, what happened in this place?

RUPA: I do not remember.

BRITISH JUSTICE

PRESENCE: There is one record of his name, in the court records in late 1859. He's been charged with incitement to stir up other farmers to refuse to sow indigo.

Under the new laws incitement is a serious offence.

(*Creating a court*) So Sadhu Charan, would have been here...
The court records we have are patchy, but there remains a partial transcript of the trial.

The PRESENCE plays a Lawyer:

LAWYER: My lord the defence has argued that the case for the prosecution rests on falsehood. Well, lawyers are well-known for lying and cheating. Their profession is to cheat. But in this case, there is a difference. Lawyers engaged by planters are compelled by planters to base their cases only on the truth. This is because planters are Christians, and falsehood is deemed to be one of the worst sins in their religion. A Christian cannot act dishonestly. He cannot even think dishonestly.

The prosecution has presented evidence of Sadhu Charan's base character, his subversion, his dishonesty.

SADHU is pained by this misrepresentation.

PRESENCE: Then there is a gap in the account, and a witness called Rashida Begum takes the stand:

RASHIDA: Sadhu Charan is...
Sadhu is well known... to be a violent type.
He often becomes involved in fights. He tries to cheat men of their money.
Once he left a man with only one eye.
He is...
He is a supporter of unrest. He talked approvingly of the agitators.
He threatened to beat me if I did not refuse to plant indigo.
I want to plant indigo, because the Planter is a good man.
I love to plant indigo.

SADHU emerges. His crown of mud has sprouted an indigo plant.

PRESENCE: The judge asks SADHU if he has anything to say in his defence, but nothing is put on the record.

YOU WILL COME TO ME TONIGHT

SADHU in a local jail. He sits there, crouched on the floor. Wearing the crown, from which now still grows the young plant. Now he is haggard and dirty.

KSHETROMANI stands above him. She too looks thin and dirty.

SADHU: You went to see Nabima Madhab?

KSHETROMANI: She was not there.
They said she has gone to the forest to become a revolutionary.

SADHU: So we cannot borrow the money?

KSHETROMANI: No.

SADHU: So we cannot pay the fine?

Pause.

KSHETROMANI: Six months for inciting against an indigo contract!

Pause.

GOPI enters. He carries some tiffin boxes. They contain food.

GOPI: I have some good news. It is his birthday. He wishes to make a gift to his farmers.

SADHU shakes his head.

GOPI: (*Of KSHETROMANI*) Then she can take it. The Saheb is worried about her.
Sadhu, I am sorry for your troubles.

SADHU: But still you serve him?

GOPI: If I stopped, how would I feed my family?
Everyone has now taken the advance.
If you took the advance, your debt would be forgotten.
Sadhu, you do not understand. There are men in Swarpur lying dead now for refusing to take it.

GOPI: Perhaps she can visit him? (*ie: ROSE*)

The Giant comes upon SADHU.

SADHU: Get out.

GOPI: Sadhu.

SADHU: Get out.

GOPI: Brother, think about it.

SADHU rushes to strike GOPI, but holds himself back at the last moment.

GOPI exits.

SADHU: *(Of the Giant)* I can see it.
How do you kill it?

KSHETROMANI: You cannot.

SADHU: There must be a way.

KSHETROMANI: There is no way.
He has his hands round your heart.
And so your heart cannot beat.

SADHU: I have heard things about you... In here.
He said he saw you walking along the river. Towards the factory.
Did you go to him?

KSHETROMANI: Of course not.

SADHU: Are you working for it? The Giant?

KSHETROMANI: No

SADHU: Are you fucking it?

KSHETROMANI: No.

SADHU: Did you bleed yet, this month?

Beat.

You came to me in my bed only once, in a month.
You should have come to me again.

He raises his arm.

You are supposed to be mine.

KSHETROMANI: I see you have been thinking in the go-down.

SADHU: Why do you give up on me?

KSHETROMANI: I do not.

SADHU: You could have helped me!

KSHETROMANI: How?

SADHU: The day you came, we have been cursed.
It is you, who has brought this on me.

Pause.

KSHETROMANI: You are right...
It's me it wants. It wants me,
It wants to destroy me.
I don't know why, but it does.
The sun shined on you until the day I arrived in your life.

Long pause.

SADHU: Will you sleep with him?
Will you love him?

KSHETROMANI: It would be easier.

SADHU: When?

KSHETROMANI: It might as well be now.

SADHU: You look so weak.

KSHETROMANI: He will feed me well. He will release you.

SADHU: Will he let me grow rice?

KSHETROMANI: He needs you to take the advance.

SADHU: Why?

KSHETROMANI: Because he knows it is YOU. He knows it is
you, he has to break.
You saw him, from the very first moment.

Pause.

SADHU: There was a night, when you were so tender with me.

KSHETROMANI: Do not think of it.

SADHU: There was love there.
Why is that over now?

KSHETROMANI looks away.

SADHU: Did you ever love me?

KSHETROMANI looks away. ROSE enters.

KSHETROMANI flees.

ROSE: (*About KSHETROMANI, as she departs*)
I want you to know that I will look after her.
I will ensure that she does not want.
And I will release you.
That is the bargain.
Do you accept it?
All this will be over

ROSE comes to take the indigo crown off, but SADHU stops him.

SADHU: No. I will keep it.

Pause.

ROSE: Tomorrow I will come to you with a contract. A deed of advance payment.
I will make an offer only to you.
I will pay you for ten first class bundles only

SADHU: How much will you pay?

ROSE: I will pay you three rupees per first-class bundle.
As with Lovegrove. You will keep the rate a secret.
But everyone will see that you have taken the advance.
I will cancel your debt to me, so long as she stays with me.

Tomorrow, Sadhu, you will be a free man.
And you will take my advance.

ROSE seizes SADHU's head. He looks in his eyes.

Maybe, one day, we can be friends.
We can sit on the verandah
And talk of soil. And hobbies.
I am not a wicked person, Sadhu.
I do not want to be.
But this is where we are.

KSHETROMANI AND NABINA

1860. A forest near Kanaipur.

NABINA: Did anyone see you?

KSHETROMANI: No.

NABINA: Are you certain?

KSHETROMANI: I was careful.

NABINA: He has his spies everywhere.

KSHETROMANI: Yes.

NABINA: How is your husband?

KSHETROMANI: He is shrinking.

NABINA: The Giants make us all shrink.
For me, too. Sometimes I feel so shrunken.
Our country—it used to be wealthy beyond imagining.

NABINA offers KSHETROMANI food and drink.

Please, eat and drink. Rice. Vegetables.

KSHETROMANI eats, hungrily.

NABINA: I heard you are part of the bargain.

KSHETROMANI: That was the price this time.

NABINA touches KSHETROMANI, gently, on her cheek.

NABINA: How do you feel?

KSHETROMANI: It doesn't matter how I feel.

NABINA: Are you angry?

KSHETROMANI: I'm too tired to be angry.

NABINA: What would you like to do to him?
There is no shame in your feelings. They are only feelings.
Do you want to harm him? Rose.
Sometimes I have fantasies about what I would do. How I
would kill him.
These thoughts are natural.
I have killed him in so many ways.
Do you want to kill him, too?
I want to tear his eyes out.
I want to cut out his tongue.
I want to cut off his hands.
I want to take him to the go-down, and bury him alive.

There is an intensity between them. Almost anything could happen now, between them.

He has brought my family almost to nothing.
They are only thoughts. Thoughts come and they go.

KSHETROMANI: Do not try and turn me like some half-wit
raiyat. This is not about my 'feelings'.

NABINA: Your anger is all you have left, now.
Bengal is a tinderbox. Something that is going to ignite.
All it needs is a spark, and many men are waiting.
Why did you come to me, if not for this?
I can see it in you. I can see how you burn.

NABINA produces a knife.

Mr Wood is visiting Rose tomorrow. If you can take them both, good. But one of them will be enough.

KSHETROMANI: I am not capable of this.

NABINA: The moment I saw your passion I knew it was you... I knew that it was you, that I wanted.

KSHETROMANI: I am nothing. I am shit.

NABINA: Why did you even come to me?
The Giant what it does, it makes us feel so small and stupid, and shit.

KSHETROMANI: You don't understand.

NABINA: I do.

KSHETROMANI: I am a curse.

NABINA: No. Kshetromani. One day, you will challenge the universe.

ACT FOUR – HOME

THE LEDGER

The PRESENCE and RUPA, by the walls of the factory. There is still a small outbuilding left over from SADHU's time—GOPI's office.

PRESENCE: There are snakes in there.

RUPA: They will not harm me.

PRESENCE: There is poison in their fangs.

RUPA: I remembered this place from when I was a child. I used to be so scared to come here.

The PRESENCE unlocks the padlock of the door. He enters.

RUPA pauses, then goes in. The PRESENCE strikes up an oil lamp.

PRESENCE: Look.

Revealed are rotting and cobwebbed shelves, on which are many ledgers.

The PRESENCE takes one down.

These are the accounts of the factory. When the factory became disused these ledgers remained, locked away.

The PRESENCE opens a ledger.

Here are the advances that were offered by the farmers in the season of 1860.
Run your finger along the records of payments.
They've almost all been filled in.
The farmers accepting the advances.

RUPA: Yes.

PRESENCE: The acceptance of this payment signaled ruination. Capitulation.

The PRESENCE sees something on the floor—ROSE's Shyamchand.

RUPA: Wait.

There's an empty box, here.

PRESENCE: Yes

They look through the ledger inside it.

RUPA: This household did not accept the advance.

PRESENCE: No, they refused it.

What was the name? Tell me, Rupa Charan, what was the name of the household?

RUPA reads the text.

RUPA: Charan. The House of Sadhu Charan.

How did they have that strength?

PRESENCE: You have to give it them.

RUPA: I don't understand.

PRESENCE: You have to go back and give it them.

You're their future.

They need to know they have a future.

The PRESENCE pulls out a bel fruit, and hands it to RUPA.

THE PLANTER'S HOUSE

The interior of ROSE's bungalow.

ROSE and KSHETROMANI. She is wearing a European frock of indigo. ROSE has dyed it himself.

ROSE: Good. It fits.

It's perfect.

She allows herself to look at herself in the mirror. Who is she? It's like she's a different person.

Do you like it?

She tries out her new self. Her new movement, her new mind, her new bearing.

Mr Wood is coming tonight, and I wish you to be at your most radiant.

I understand this is not how you would want it.

You will never be in hardship again.

KSHETROMANI: And Sadhu?

ROSE: Why should you care about Sadhu anymore?

Pause.

She smiles.

I'm going to come over to you now.

But you mustn't be scared.

It's just that we do not understand each other yet.

Pause.

He puts his hand out to her.

I don't want a struggle.

I'm not going to force you.

That's not who I am.

She considers falling into him.

I don't think you understand me, yet.

I am not evil.

There is nothing wrong in my soul.

I want to love, just like you.

I want to be happy, just like you.

I want you.

I can't help it. I am in love with you.

Do you love me?

I wonder if you'll say it to me. Will you tell me 'I love you.'

Pause.

KSHETROMANI: I love you.

ROSE: Will you say it in Bangla.

KSHETROMANI: (*In Bangla*) I love you.

She makes to touch his feet.

ROSE: Please. I remember, when you touched my feet, in your house
I felt so ashamed.
I don't want to have power over you.
I want you to have power over me.
I want you to come to me.

ROSE becomes frustrated.

A Kokil cries outside.

What was that?

She calls back to it. It gives her strength. He goes over to the window.

She takes a knife from the table. She has the opportunity to kill him with it. She approaches him. He turns round. He sees her with the knife. A look of alarm on him. But then, without batting an eyelid, she takes the bel fruit from the bowl and cracks it open.

She smells it. She puts her fingers into the flesh, and eats some.

ROSE watches her with all his desire.

ROSE: I want to plant something inside you.

KSHETROMANI: You cannot.

ROSE: Why not?

KSHETROMANI: Already there is a child in there
His child.

ROSE: You cannot bear his child.

KSHETROMANI: I will.

ROSE: We can take it out.

The Kokil calls.

ROSE: That noise!

KSHETROMANI: I am protected.

He lays a hand on her, gripping her frock.

She pulls away, ripping the frock.

Then she rips it again, with an extraordinary strength, refashioning it (as a dhoti? A sari?), until it is her own garment.

ROSE: You people. Why do you make me feel that there is something wrong with me? There is nothing wrong with me.

KSHETROMANI: You are just a boy in a foreign land.
I do not know if there is something wrong with you.
But there is something wrong with (*of the whole indigo system, of colonialism*) with all this. Come, if you want anything more, you will have to use violence, now.

ROSE goes to a table, and picks up his shyamchand.

He raises it.

The PRESENCE enters, unseen.

ROSE approaches her with his shyamchand raised. He pushes her against the wall.

ROSE: I have wondered, in idle moments, what it would be like to force the death of someone. I think Sadhu will die. He has suicide in his head.
Perhaps he has already gone.

But when ROSE tries to move close to her again, he is prevented, as if she is protected by an invisible force.

KSHETROMANI: You will not win.
You will kill us but you will not win.
There is something in us that is so strong.
In the end this land will rise up.
And then it will be over for you.

THE BEL FRUIT

SADHU's field.

SADHU is digging a trench in the ground.

We realise he is digging his own grave.

Then, he finds some thin rope. It is already knotted into a noose. He tosses the

noose over the branch of the bel tree, then ties the other end around the tree,

so that the noose is at a suitable height.

The stump is below the noose.

He stands on the stump and puts his head in the noose.

He considers jumping.

He closes his eyes.

SADHU: Are you there?
Are you there?

This is what you want, isn't it?
This is what you want.
Is this permitted, master?
Now you have her, am I free?
I do not think so.

When I am dead, you will take my land.
And even if they scatter my ashes here, you will not permit me
to haunt the fields.

The Kokil calls.

SADHU is distracted by it for a moment.

The PRESENCE enters.

With his head in the noose, SADHU pulls at the rope above him, to test the tension. He does it again.

As he pulls, a bel fruit falls to the ground.

A bel?

Pause.

He tugs at the rope again, and another fruit falls.

He gets down off the stump and goes to the bel fruit. He opens it up with his kazla to reveal its strange flesh. He savours the smell of the fruit. He eats the fruit.

Someone begins to sing a song.

CHORUS: The leaves of the Neel plant are green
But a paddy is greener
The green of the paddy field
Lives in my heart
To whom I sacrifice my life
I sacrifice my life

The PRESENCE gives SADHU a vision of SADHU's land that is overflowing and bountiful—rows and rows of various plants, trees, full of colour and bounty.

PRESENCE: This will belong to your children.
All this will belong to them.

SADHU: When?

PRESENCE: Soon enough.

SADHU: For how long?

PRESENCE: Only for a time.
But time enough for happiness.

The PRESENCE brings out a bag of seed. SADHU takes a handful.

The PRESENCE evens out the earth—so you could plant in it.

PRESENCE: She is coming. She is powerful. Hold on. Only hold on a moment.

KSHETROMANI enters.

SADHU: What happened?

KSHETROMANI: I did not give him what he wanted.

She goes to the tree. She sees the noose.

KSHETROMANI: You decided not to?

SADHU: A bel fruit fell.
And it scared the giant away, for a moment.
Here.

He hands the fruit to her.

Taste it.

She tastes it.

SADHU: (*Of the hanging*) It's too much.
I do not have it within me.
I do not have the courage.

He starts to cry.

I'm ignorant and rough.
I'm a burning shitheap.

Pause.

KSHETROMANI: You are kind. You are gentle. You make me
    feel welcome.
    You are a cultivator.
    Everything you touch grows strong.
    And green.
    Everything you plant will become mighty.
    Their roots will go deep in the earth.
    One day, what you have planted will blossom.

    Our land wants you. It needs you. What you do is blessed. You
    know what is right for it.
    I am sorry, Sadhu, but he will come for you.
    He will be here for you by the morning.

SADHU makes up his mind about something. He starts to even the ground.

KSHETROMANI: What are you doing?

SADHU: Planting.

KSHETROMANI: At this hour?

He takes the mattock and starts to dig

KSHETROMANI: Sadhu, what are doing?

SADHU: (*Of a seed*) I will put this, in the soil.

KSHETROMANI: What is it?

SADHU: A surprise.

KSHETROMANI: So what will you do?

SADHU: I will work all night.

KSHETROMANI: You will flood the fields?

SADHU: Yes.

KSHETROMANI: How long will it be before they notice?

SADHU: I think a week.

KSHETROMANI: And then?

SADHU: And then we trust.

KSHETROMANI: In what?

The Kokil sings.

SADHU sings back.

SADHU: We cannot do this alone.

KSHETROMANI: We are not alone, now.
Can you hear the kokil?
It will protect us.

At the top of his voice, he hollers:

SADHU: Hoy! Rashida bundi!
Hoy Rashida!

SADHU's voice echoes over the fields. SADHU starts to sing. It is gorgeous.

Now I plough deep into soil
In hope of seeing her again.

RASHIDA enters. SADHU stops singing.

I want to tell you something.
I am telling you because I trust you.

RASHIDA looks at him.

Do you understand what I am doing?

Pause.

They will come for me.
They will accuse me of breaking a contract.
They will probably beat me to death right here.
But we have had enough.
We have had enough of feeling like we do.
In this land, we will overcome.
Something will rise up.

Tell people you trust. In five days gather the village here and they will see what I have done.

RASHIDA nods. SADHU starts to sing again. He sings with KHETROMANI.

Now I plough deep into soil
In hope of seeing her again.

MIDNIGHT

An indigo atelier in fields of green. There are gorgeous swathes of blue everywhere.

JEREMY and RUPA.

JEREMY: Hello.

RUPA: Hello.

They stare at each other.

JEREMY: You have been protesting against our company, and
    inciting others to protest.
    Demanding wage increases.
    Shorter shifts.
    Safer workplaces.
    Better management practices.
    That's fine.
    I understand.
    That's what people will do.
    And better ecological practices too.
    I think you should be commended for that.

    I'm not here to tell you to stop protesting.
    But
    This country...
    I mean, I've been coming here for 15 years and I have to tell
    you something is happening here, now.
    Everything is accelerating.

It's tremendously exciting to see so many people pulled out of poverty.
A booming middle-class
They've built a metro in Dhaka.
There are highways and freeways.
You've got a smartphone in your hands.
You can order pizza on that phone and it will be with you in 15 minutes!

I honestly...
I honestly want my business to be good for your country.
I honestly do. My business will make your country, a great nation.
We can talk about the money you're asking for. I understand you are concerned about safety, about Union rights.
We have insisted on so many changes to practise since...

But I think you should know there's always going to be a bottom line.
But this is the only way to prosperity in your country.
This is the only way.
You have to be cheap. We value your skills.
But you have to be cheap.

RUPA: I am not cheap.
I am not small.

You do not know what I can do.
You do not know my brains and my hands.
That I understand the molecular structure of indigo.
That I can work indigo so much better than you can.
You do not know I have the designs for new kinds of denim.

You do not know my capacity to organise, and lead.
We have a vision.

We will work together.
We will do it ourselves
Our own collective.
Our blue will be deeper than the night sky.

It will last forever
Here. Look.

She takes it out.

It makes London Midnight look like dishwater.

And you will take my price.
Or we will take it elsewhere.

We are not small.
We are not cheap.

We will challenge the universe.

SADHU CHARAN IS PLANTING RICE AND
THE BATTLE OF KANAIPUR

The Clay Land.

PRESENCE: In the spring of 1860, a battle takes places between
mercenaries sent by the factory, carrying lathials—and the
villagers, who armed themselves with domestic implements,
stones, gulti bricks, baellon, earthen pots, but also woodapple,
otherwise know as bel, as hard as cannon shot. The odds
were stacked against them, but somehow the villagers were
successful in repelling the mercenaries. Afterwards it was
claimed that the village had received a divine intervention.

That the ground had seemed to roar and split, to swallow up
the lathials, as if clay arms were pulling them into the mud.

We suddenly become aware that the weather is becoming turbulent, and strange.

Indigo-water begins spilling out. A storm begins.

From the village only one person fell.

SADHU lies murdered in a flooded paddy field. KSHETROMANI holds him.

Pause.

RASHIDA runs in, holding a lamp. She has not seen SADHU.

RASHIDA: Hoy Sadhu Charan! We've beaten them! We've beaten them!

RASHIDA sees SADHU. She is stunned. KSHETROMANI looks up.

KSHETROMANI: They killed him.

RASHIDA: No!

KSHETROMANI: The Lathials have killed him.
They dragged him out here, and beat him to death.

RASHIDA suddenly bellows, so loud it is as if it has been amplified for the whole world.

RASHIDA: Hoy! Sadhu Charan has been murdered!

Another villager enters.

VILLAGER: Oh no!

RASHIDA: Hoy! Sadhu Charan has been killed! Tell everyone to come.

The VILLAGER dashes off.

Just then, the sun rises. And as far as the eye can see, the paddy fields are flooded.

KSHETROMANI: Look.

RASHIDA: What?

KSHETROMANI: Look.

RASHIDA: (*In wonder*) Oh...
He was planting rice?

KSHETROMANI: Look how many people have done it?

RASHIDA: Torap, Mr Lal, Nikhil Biswas! As far as I can see, all the fields are flooded!

ROSE enters. He witnesses what is occurring.

Some villagers starts to arrive. RASHIDA starts to shout.

RASHIDA: Hoy! Sadhu Charan has planted rice!
Sadhu Charan has planted rice!

VILLAGER: Sadhu Charan has planted rice!
Sadhu Charan has planted rice!

THE FACTORY

The past melts away as now RUPA stands in the middle of the storm. She is watching the factory.

Thunder and lightning.

Then there is a terrible roar, as if from some unchained beast.

There is a great crack in the factory.

Indigo dye spills everywhere, spills in the river.

Another thunderous roar, as if from an unchained beast.

She watches it.

A figure emerges, a figure composed of vegetation. A green man. Or a green woman, plants growing out of them.

They are bloodied with blue. Is this Krishna? Is this SADHU? KSHETROMANI? Who is this?

RUPA holds their gaze.

CHORUS: On a Fortunate day
Dipped in blue of the Neel tree
On a Cuckoo calling morning
Good days will surely come back
Let the good days come back.
Let them come back.

নীল গাছের রঙে নীলা
(NEEL GACHHER RONGEY NEELA)
পয়মন্ত দিনে
(POYMONTO DINEY)
কোকিল ডাকা ভোরে
(KOKIL DAKA BHOREY)
আসবি সুদিন ফিরে
(ASHBI SHUDIN PHIREY)
ফের আসুক সুদিন ফিরে
(PHER ASHUK SHUDIN PHIREY)
ফের আসুক সুদিন ফিরে।।
(PHER ASHUK SHUDIN PHIREY)

THE END

ALSO AVAILABLE FROM SALAMANDER STREET

All Salamander Street plays can be bought in bulk at a discount for performance or study. Contact info@salamanderstreet.com to enquire about performance licenses.

OUTLIER by Malaika Kegode
ISBN: 9781914228339

Genre-defying and emotional, *Outlier* is a powerful play exploring the impact of isolation, addiction and friendship on young people in often-forgotten places.

CHATSKY & MISER, MISER! by Anthony Burgess
ISBN: 9781914228889

Anthony Burgess expertly tackles the major monuments of French and Russian theatre: *The Miser* by Molière and *Chatsky* by Alexander Griboyedov. Burgess's verse and prose plays Chatsky: The Importance of Being Stupid and Miser, Miser! are published for the first time in this volume.

SORRY WE DIDN'T DIE AT SEA
by Emanuele Aldrovandi translated by Marco Young
ISBN: 9781914228964

A darkly absurdist comedy offers a refracted story of European migration, asking how well we would fare if we were forced to make a perilous journey across the sea, and what lengths we would go to in order to survive.

GROUP PORTRAIT IN A SUMMER LANDSCAPE
by Peter Arnott
ISBN: 9781914228933

An intense and riveting play set in a Perthshire country house during the Scottish Independence referendum of 2014. A retired academic and political heavyweight invites family and former students together for a dramatic reckoning.

PLACEHOLDER by Catherine Bisset
ISBN: 9781914228919

Profoundly thought-provoking, this solo play about the historical actor-singer of colour known as 'Minette' offers an exploration of the complex racial and social dynamics of what would become the first independent nation in the Caribbean.

Printed in the USA
CPSIA information can be obtained
at www.ICGtesting.com
JSHW01205614O824
68134JS00035B/3473

9 781738 429332